This book belongs to

_____

GROWTH & STUDY GUIDE

FINDING
GOD'S
PATH
THROUGH YOUR
TRIALS

Elizabeth George

HARVEST HOUSE PUBLISHERS

EUGENE, OREGON

Cover photo © Gary Yeowell / Photographer's Choice / Getty Images

Cover by Dugan Design Group, Bloomington, Minnesota

Acknowledgments

As always, thank you to my dear husband, Jim George, M.Div., Th.M., for your able assistance, guidance, suggestions, and loving encouragement on this project.

FINDING GOD'S PATH THROUGH YOUR TRIALS GROWTH AND STUDY GUIDE
Copyright © 2007 by Elizabeth George
Published by Harvest House Publishers
Eugene, Oregon 97402
www.harvesthousepublishers.com

ISBN-13: 978-0-7369-1652-3
ISBN-10: 0-7369-1652-0

Printed in the United States of America

07 08 09 10 11 12 13 14 15 / VP-SK / 12 11 10 9 8 7 6 5 4 3 2 1

Contents

Section 4—Becoming a Mighty Woman

Section 5—Becoming an Enduring Woman

A Final Word

From My Heart to Yours

❦

❦ We all face trials, and I'm sorry you're hurting. Unfortunately, trials are a fact of life here on earth. But God is with us! He promises to give us the strength and support we need to persevere to the end of the difficulty. And on top of that, He says He will use our trials to help us grow into the people He created us to be. As we begin this journey of better understanding God and how to find and stay on His path for us, I pray the main book, *Finding God's Path Through Your Trials*, and this growth and study guide will be extremely helpful and practical for you and others. We'll explore six powerful promises from God and how to integrate them into our lives. We can have hope and direction as we walk through our difficult times with Him!

Joy Is Coming

The lessons in this growth and study guide are easy to follow and do. You'll need a copy of *Finding God's Path Through Your Trials*, a Bible, and a heart ready to discover and implement God's wisdom in navigating trials. After you read the chapter in the

main book, the questions, insights, and additional scriptures in
this growth and study guide will give you a better understanding
of the truths found in the Bible that can help you face, persevere,
and triumph in any and every trial, however great and small.

Although it may sound almost impossible now, in the book
of James, the author encourages you to count your trials as joy.
Through this study, you'll explore this concept and how you can
have God's joy in the midst of your problems. You'll also find
time-tested strategies for successfully handling personal sorrows,
issues, and challenges.

The Advantages of Group Study

You will grow spiritually as you work your way through and
apply the biblical principles presented in this growth and study
guide, but I urge you to share this rich and life-changing journey
with others—your friends, your neighbors, your Sunday school
class, your Bible study. No matter how small or large the group,
the personal care and interest shared will be uplifting and sup-
portive. Your sisters-in-Christ will pray for you, and you for them.
You'll have a mutual exchange of experiences. And you'll have
accountability, along with some healthy peer pressure. This helps
motivate you to do the lessons and experience glorious spiritual
growth! There is sweet, sweet encouragement as you share God's
Word with one another and stimulate one another to greater love
and good works.

If you feel guided by God to lead a study group, I've included
a section in the back of this study guide entitled "Leading a Bible
Study Discussion Group." This practical, hands-on information…
and more…is also available on my website:

www.ElizabethGeorge.com

Reaping the Benefits of Following God's Path

If you use the truths and the promises from God's Word that are spotlighted in the main book, *Finding God's Path Through Your Trials,* and in this exciting study guide, by God's grace and with His help, you will make it through your troubles without becoming overwhelmed or experiencing...

❧ anxiety	❧ discouragement
❧ bitterness	❧ fear
❧ blaming	❧ hopelessness
❧ depression	❧ worry

You—yes, you!—can know the inner joy, growth, and maturity that comes when you follow God's path for successfully handling every difficulty you face now and in the future. Experience God's peace and joy today!

In His everlasting love,

Elizabeth George

1

Accepting the Truth

❦

My brethren, count it all joy
when you fall into various trials.
JAMES 1:2

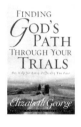

Read chapter 1, "Accepting the Truth," in *Finding God's Path Through Your Trials.* Note any new truths or challenges that stand out to you.

God has wisdom and practical help for you as you face your everyday difficulties, whether they're surprises or ongoing challenges. What is the Number One problem you face today? Write it down and add what instructions God has for you.

HIDING GOD'S WORD IN YOUR HEART

Memorize James 1:2. Write down how it appears in your favorite
Bible version. You may want to look at a few other translations
and note any words that differ or help you better understand the
meaning of this verse.

Looking to Another Teacher

Jot down what these scriptures reveal about James' background,
character, and ministry.

Matthew 13:53-56 and Galatians 1:19—

John 7:5—

Acts 12:17—

Acts 15:13—

Acts 21:17-18—

1 Corinthians 15:7—

James' epistle addresses the external and internal problems believers were facing—their trials and testings. Externally these saints were...

persecuted—

oppressed—

displaced—

Do any of these conditions describe your life at present? If so, put a checkmark by the appropriate word(s) just listed and give a brief description of your trial.

As a result of these external problems, there were also internal problems, such as:

spiritual distress—

wrong doctrine—

wrong living patterns—

a low spiritual state—

wrong attitudes toward God—

Are you currently suffering from any of these states? If so, put a checkmark by the appropriate word(s) and give a brief description of your trial.

The recipients of James' letter allowed their conditions to lead to personal problems, which in turn led to...

unbridled speech—

strife—

factions—

worldliness—

Put a checkmark by any of these problem areas that are currently part of your everyday life and give a brief example.

Getting Straight to the Point

How do you normally handle trials?

❧ What command did James have in James 1:2 for his readers... and for you?

❧ What command did Paul have in Philippians 4:4 for his readers...and for you?

Trials Are a Fact of Life

What word does James use to indicate that trials are a fact of life?

What did Jesus say about trials and hardships in John 16:33?

And Paul in Acts 14:22?

And in 2 Timothy 3:12?

And Peter in 1 Peter 1:7?

And in 1 Peter 4:12?

Learning to Count

Read these verses and make notes about what stands out to you.

2 Corinthians 4:16-18—

2 Corinthians 5:7—

How do these scriptures encourage you to count trials as joy when they may not look like joy or feel like joy…and you can't imagine how they could ever have any joy in them?

–Taking a Step Forward–

Read this section in your book again. Write out the step or steps you were asked to take to experience joy in your trials…to become a joyful woman. Feel free to add any additional steps or ideas you think of.

As you consider the contents of this chapter and the joy you can experience in your trials, place a check mark by the step or steps you will take today. What difference will doing this step(s) make concerning your trials?

Be joyful!

2

Using an Easy Sorting System

> *Consider it all joy, my brethren,*
> *when you encounter various trials.*
> JAMES 1:2 NASB

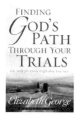

Read chapter 2, "Using an Easy Sorting System," in *Finding God's Path Through Your Trials*. Note any new truths or challenges that stand out to you.

God has wisdom and practical help for you as you face your everyday difficulties, whether they're surprises or ongoing challenges. What is the Number One problem you face today? Write it down and add what instructions God has for you.

The Bookkeeping Principle

Take a minute to look at your checkbook register and notice the two columns there. One is probably entitled "debit" and the other "credit." How would you describe the difference? (You may want to use your dictionary.)

Debit or Credit?

Imagine that every time you experience a trial you must make a decision about which column to place your trial into. These are your choices:

Column 1	Column 2
credit	debit
income	expense
asset	loss
joy	sorrow

⅔ Which column does James instruct us to choose?

⅔ What difference do you think following James' instruction will make in your outlook toward trials?

Reacting or Yielding?

Look at these scriptures and note their promises.

Psalm 34:9 —

Psalm 34:10 —

Psalm 84:11 —

Proverbs 10:22 —

Matthew 7:7-11 —

In a few words, write out the main message from this group of verses.

Spend a few moments writing down your thoughts about how these promises encourage your choice to yield rather than react when you face a trial.

Doing It Daily

By now you realize spiritual bookkeeping must be done on a daily basis.

❧ What trial are you facing today or this week?

❧ Through prayer, place your trial in the "Joy" column and describe how it can become a credit, income, asset.

❧ What change of heart do you experience as you follow God's bookkeeping rule to count your trial as joy?

Persevering Through Pain

Describe the suffering of these two men.

Job (Job 1:13-19)—

Paul (2 Corinthians 11:22-28)—

♾ How does their suffering compare with the pain, suffering, and heartache you are experiencing right now?

♾ Now describe how Job and Paul responded to God as a result of their trials.

Job 1:21 —

2 Corinthians 12:9 —

♾ In your own words, what is the best way to handle your trials? And how will you apply this to your current situation?

−Taking a Step Forward−

Read this section in your book again. Write out the step or steps you were asked to take to experience joy in your trials…to become a joyful woman. Feel free to add any additional steps or ideas you think of.

As you consider the contents of this chapter and the joy you can experience in your trials, place a check mark by the step or steps you will take today. What difference will doing this step(s) make concerning your trials?

Be joyful!

3

Evaluating What's Happening

❧

*Consider it pure joy, my brothers, whenever
you face trials of many kinds.*

JAMES 1:2 NIV

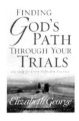

Read chapter 3, "Evaluating What's Happening," in
Finding God's Path Through Your Trials. Note any
new truths or challenges that stand out to you.

God has wisdom and practical help for you as you face your
everyday difficulties, whether they're surprises or ongoing challenges. What is the Number One problem you face today? Write
it down and add what instructions God has for you.

Viewing Trials the Wrong Way

Look over the list of misconceptions about trials in this section. Write down those that describe *your* views about your trials.

If you're like the rest of us, you've been guilty of viewing trials the wrong way. What have you learned so far about looking at your trials from God's perspective?

Knowing Genuine Joy

In sharing God's wisdom, James points out that when you do your spiritual bookkeeping, you are to count your trials as "all" joy. Consider these translations of the joy available in each and every trial. Check your favorite.

___ pure joy

___ nothing but joy

___ greatest joy

___ wholly joy

___ unreserved joy

Hebrews 11:1 says, "Faith is the substance of things hoped for, the evidence of things not seen." How does this help you see your problems as joy through "eyes of faith"?

Rejoicing No Matter What

Put your imagination to work as you read through Paul's list of pain, sufferings, and heartache in 2 Corinthians 11:23-29. Then answer the following questions.

How many times was Paul beaten with 39 stripes?

How frequently was he beaten with rods?

How often was he stoned?

How many times was he shipwrecked?

What burden came upon him daily?

While Paul was in prison and on death row, he wrote to suffering Christians in Philippi about the right attitude for enduring pain and persecution. In your own words, what did he prescribe in these verses?

Philippians 1:18—

Philippians 3:1—

Philippians 3:3—

Philippians 4:4—

Philippians 4:9—

—Taking a Step Forward—

Read this section in your book again. Write out the step or steps you were asked to take to experience joy in your trials…to become a joyful woman. Feel free to add any additional steps or ideas you think of.

As you consider the contents of this chapter and the joy you can experience in your trials, place a check mark by the step or steps you will take today. What difference do you think taking this step(s) will make concerning your trials?

Be joyful!

4

Expecting Bumps, Roadblocks, and Dead Ends

*Dear brothers and sisters, whenever trouble comes
your way, let it be an opportunity for joy.*
JAMES 1:2 NLT

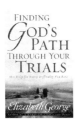

Read chapter 4, "Expecting Bumps, Roadblocks, and Dead Ends" in *Finding God's Path Through Your Trials*. Note any new truths or challenges that stand out to you.

God has wisdom and practical help for you as you face your everyday difficulties, whether they're surprises or ongoing challenges. What is the Number One problem you face today? Write it down and add what instructions God has for you.

Walking Through Your Ordeals

If acceptance is the bottom-line response to your problems, how are you dealing with your Number One problem?

What does the instruction in Galatians 5:16 tell you about handling your ordeals, including your Number One problem?

According to verse 22, what happens when you follow this command?

Read again Tim Hansel's description of his process of learning to deal with pain.

What insights into your own trials do you gain from his experience?

Do you agree or disagree that joy is a choice? Why or why not?

Encountering Trials

When instructing you about trials, James writes about the way of trials. We "fall into" them (NKJV), "encounter" them (NASB), or "face them" (NIV). The word translated in these various ways is the same term used in the story about the Good Samaritan in Luke 10:30-35. Take a minute to read that story now.

❧ What does verse 30 say happened to this man as he was going about his business?

❧ Share a trial you "encountered" or "fell into" or "faced" this week.

❧ Instead of being surprised when trials come your way, what should you do each day to prepare for the sure-to-come trials?

Experiencing a Variety of Trials

Fill in the blank:

"My brethren, count it all joy when you fall into _____ trials."

❧ Using a dictionary, write out a definition of the word "various."

In 2 Corinthians 11 Paul reports the variety of trials he fell into. Now it's your turn. Look back over the past few months—or years—and briefly describe a few of your own.

❧ God promised Paul—and you!—that His grace is sufficient for any and all varieties of trials. Look at 2 Corinthians 12:9. How did you experience the truth and promise of God's grace in your own trials? When you're finished writing out the ways, pause and give God thanks!

—Taking a Step Forward—

Read this section in your book again. Write out the step or steps you were asked to take to experience joy in your trials…to become a joyful woman. Feel free to add any additional steps or ideas you think of.

As you consider the contents of this chapter and the joy you can experience in your trials, place a check mark by the step or steps you will take today. What difference do you think taking this step(s) will make concerning your trials?

Be joyful!

5

Looking for Blessings

❧

Knowing that the testing of your faith
produces patience.
JAMES 1:3

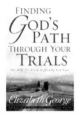
Read chapter 5, "Looking for Blessings," in *Finding God's Path Through Your Trials*. Note any new truths or challenges that stand out to you.

God has wisdom and practical help for you as you face your everyday difficulties, whether they're surprises or ongoing challenges. What is the Number One problem you face today? Write it down and add what instructions God has for you.

HIDING GOD'S WORD IN YOUR HEART

Memorize James 1:3. Write down how it appears in your favorite Bible version. You may want to look at a few other translations and note any words that differ or help you better understand the meaning of this verse.

Hearing God's Good News

After informing his readers (and you) about the reality of trials in James 1:2, James now has some good news: Trials produce patience and endurance! Using a dictionary, jot down some brief and simple definitions of the following words:

Patient—

Enduring—

Persistent—

Constant—

Steadfast—

Faithful—

Steady—

All of these words describe the Christian whose faith has been tested. Circle the one you like most and briefly explain why.

Trials are for "testing" your faith. According to these scriptures, what are some qualities God desires for your faith?

Matthew 15:28—

Romans 4:19-20—

1 Timothy 1:5—

2 Timothy 1:5—

On a scale of 1 to 5 (5 being greatest), rate your faith and trust in God...and explain why.

According to James 1:3 how is faith grown?

Under what conditions was faith grown in these scriptures?

2 Corinthians 1:3-4—

Hebrews 11:17—

1 Peter 1:7—

Using James 1:3, write a brief prayer to God expressing your desire to grow in faith.

Sketching Out Staying Power

The Christian whose faith has been tested and who endures through that testing reaps a benefit that can be gained in no other way: staying power. According to these scriptures, what are some of the stepping-stones on God's path through trials that result in staying power?

1 Thessalonians 2:14—

1 Thessalonians 3:3-4—

2 Thessalonians 1:4—

James 5:11—

The apostle Paul's life is an example of staying power...of endurance and patience. Check out these verses to find out some of the ways his endurance and patience were developed.

Acts 9:15-16: The Lord is describing Paul in these verses. What was Paul's job assignment from God?

Acts 16:26: While Paul was suffering and "staying" in prison, what did God do?

Acts 18:9-10: While Paul was suffering and "staying" in Corinth, what did God do?

2 Timothy 4:16-18: While Paul was again suffering and "staying" in his legal trial, what did God do?

What do these examples from Paul's life teach you about staying in your trials even when suffering…about staying faithful through your trials?

What are some ways you generally try (or at least think about trying) to get yourself out of suffering?

How do you tend to manipulate your situation to keep from going through trials?

What blessings are you forfeiting when you avoid staying in your trials?

Pen a prayer to God purposing to develop greater staying power so you can reap the benefits of finding His path *through* your trials.

Looking to the End

What two practices were suggested in this section to help you make it through each day?

Suggestion 1—

Suggestion 2—

What benefits do these scriptures reveal about persevering through your trials?

Romans 5:3-4—

Romans 8:28—

2 Corinthians 4:17-18—

−Taking a Step Forward−

Read this section in your book again. Write out the step or steps you were asked to take to gain constancy and patience in your trials…to become a stable woman. Feel free to add any additional steps or ideas you think of.

As you consider the contents of this chapter and the stability you gain as a result of your trials, place a check mark by the step or steps you will take today. What difference do you think taking this step(s) will make concerning your trials?

Press forward for the prize!

6

Changing Your Perspective

ैं

*Knowing that the testing of your faith
produces endurance.*

JAMES 1:3 NASB

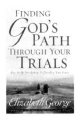

Read chapter 6, "Changing Your Perspective," in *Finding God's Path Through Your Trials*. Note any new truths or challenges that stand out to you.

God has wisdom and practical help for you as you face your everyday difficulties, whether they're surprises or ongoing challenges. What is the Number One problem you face today? Write it down and add what instructions God has for you.

Standing Up Under Pressure

At times we all fail to stand up under pressure, but God is faithful and patient to continue the process of strengthening our faith in Him and our staying power in our trials. Read the stories of these three people who initially failed to stand up under pressure but later were used mightily by God.

&# *Samson*

What was God's mission for Samson as told to his parents (Judges 13:5)?

What actions did Samson take that revealed he was not standing up under pressure according to…

Judges 14:1-3—

Judges 16:1—

Judges 16:4—

How did Samson ultimately pass God's test (Judges 16:28)?

❧ *Peter*

What actions did Peter take that revealed he was not standing up under pressure (Mark 14:66-72)?

How did Peter ultimately pass God's test (Acts 2:14-24)?

❧ *John Mark*

What actions did John Mark take that revealed he was not standing up under pressure (Acts 13:5 and 13)?

How do we know John Mark ultimately passed God's test (2 Timothy 4:11)?

Remaining Strong Through Affliction

James reminds us that testing strengthens our faith and trust in God. Sarah lived during Old Testament times. She's mentioned in Hebrews 11, which indicates she was a woman of great faith. Note how Sarah's faith was tested in each of these scriptures.

Genesis 12:5—

Genesis 15:2—

Genesis 16:1—

Genesis 17:17—

Defining Faith

What does Ephesians 2:8-9 say about the relationship between grace and faith with respect to salvation (saving faith)?

Read again the description of *genuine saving faith* in your book. Briefly define "faith" in your own words.

Proving Your Faith

What did you learn is *not* being tested when you fall into various trials?

How was this helpful to you in developing rocklike character?

Others Whose Faith Was Tested

How did each of these women exhibit trust in God?

❧ *Noah's wife* (Genesis 7:1-7)—

❧ *Rebekah* (Genesis 24:48-58)—

❧ *Miriam* (Exodus 14:10-22)—

❧ *Ruth* (Ruth 1:15-17)—

❧ *The widow of Zarephath* (1 Kings 17:10-15)—

❧ *Esther* (Esther 4:11-16)—

❧ *Elizabeth* (Luke 1:6-7)—

How do these women encourage you in your own actions
and decisions?

–Taking a Step Forward–

Read this section in your book again. Write out the step or steps you were asked to take to gain constancy and patience in your trials...to become a stable woman. Feel free to add any additional steps or ideas you think of.

As you consider the contents of this chapter and the stability you gain as a result of your trials, place a check mark by the step or steps you will take today. What difference do you think taking this step(s) will make concerning your trials?

Press forward for the prize!

7

Strengthening Your Staying Power

> *You know that the testing of your faith develops perseverance.*
> JAMES 1:3 NIV

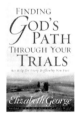

Read chapter 7, "Strengthening Your Staying Power," in *Finding God's Path Through Your Trials*. Note any new truths or challenges that stand out to you.

God has wisdom and practical help for you as you face your everyday difficulties, whether they're surprises or ongoing challenges. What is the Number One problem you face today? Write it down and add what instructions God has for you.

Growing in Patience

Accomplishing God's purposes is a benefit derived from enduring through trials. Look at the suffering of our Savior in Matthew 27:38-44. What is the scene?

In your own words, what were the people asking of Jesus?

Why do you think Jesus did not come down from the cross?

What did Christ accomplish by enduring through this trial, by staying on the cross?

Look at the suffering of the apostle Paul in Acts 21:8-14. What is the scene? What was the prophecy?

In your own words, what were the people asking of Paul?

What was Paul's response (verse 13)?

Clearly Christ and Paul had a God-perspective on their lives and trials. What lessons can you learn from them about suffering and fulfilling God's purposes? About personal comfort versus fulfilling God's will?

Think about your current trial or difficult situation. How do the examples of Jesus and Paul encourage you?

The Power of Rewards

External rewards are helpful, but the ultimate reward comes from tapping into God's power and handling your trials His way. List several rewards Peter mentions for staying through your trials (1 Peter 1:6-9).

Producing a Harvest of Virtues

Patience (endurance) produces an abundance of virtues. As you stay in your trials, these virtues add strength to your ability to handle your trials.

❧ *Confidence*—Where did Paul say you can find confidence (Philippians 1:6)?

❧ *Courage*—Where did Paul say you can find courage (Philippians 4:13)?

❧ *Constancy*—Where did Paul say you can find constancy (2 Corinthians 9:8 and 12:9)?

How does this encourage you in your...

...pain?

...tiredness?

...illness?

...unhappiness?

❧ Christlikeness—Look at 2 Peter 1:5-7. Which of these virtues do you need to faithfully nurture and add to your lifestyle to mirror Christlikeness?

What will your reward be (verse 8)?

−Taking a Step Forward−

Read this section in your book again. Write out the step or steps you were asked to take to gain constancy and patience in your trials…to become a stable woman. Feel free to add any additional steps or ideas you think of.

As you consider the contents of this chapter and the stability you gain as a result of your trials, place a check mark by the step or steps you will take today. What difference do you think taking this step(s) will make concerning your trials?

Press forward for the prize!

8

Standing with the Giants of Faith

❧

For when your faith is tested, your endurance has a chance to grow.

JAMES 1:3 NLT

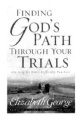

Read chapter 8, "Standing with the Giants of Faith," in *Finding God's Path Through Your Trials.* Note any new truths or challenges that stand out to you.

God has wisdom and practical help for you as you face your everyday difficulties, whether they're surprises or ongoing challenges. What is the Number One problem you face today? Write it down and add what instructions God has for you.

God's Faithful Heroes

Read Hebrews 11. How does this chapter describe the evidence of faith in the following heroes of the faith?

❧ Abel—

❧ Enoch—

❧ Noah—

❧ Abraham—

❧ Sarah—

❧ Isaac, Jacob, and Joseph—

❧ Moses—

❧ Rahab—

❧ Saints of power and authority—

❧ Numerous nameless saints—

MAKING IT PERSONAL

Look again at Hebrews 11:11.

❧ How was Sarah's faith tested?

What role did faith play?

Where did Sarah place her faith, and why?

Reflect on your own faith and trust in God. How do you tend to…

…view God's promises?

...view God?

...respond to waiting?

How does Sarah's example encourage you to endure your own testing, both present and future?

—Taking a Step Forward—

Read this section in your book again. Write out the step or steps you were asked to take to gain constancy and patience in your trials...to become a stable woman. Feel free to add any additional steps or ideas you think of.

As you consider the contents of this chapter and the stability you gain as a result of your trials, place a check mark by the step or steps you will take today. What difference do you think taking this step(s) will make concerning your trials?

Press forward for the prize!

9

Crossing over to Greatness

Let patience have its perfect work,
that you may be perfect and complete,
lacking nothing.

JAMES 1:4

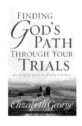

Read chapter 9, "Crossing over to Greatness," in *Finding God's Path Through Your Trials.* Note any new truths or challenges that stand out to you.

God has wisdom and practical help for you as you face your everyday difficulties, whether they're surprises or ongoing challenges. What is the Number One problem you face today? Write it down and add what instructions God has for you.

HIDING GOD'S WORD IN YOUR HEART

Memorize James 1:4. Write down how it appears in your favorite Bible version. You may want to look at a few other translations and note any words that differ or help you better understand the meaning of this verse.

Looking into a Mirror

As we begin this new section, take a look at your life, your problems, and your manner of handling your trials. Also reflect on what you've learned about finding God's path through your trials so far.

❧ What progress have you made in the way you are handling your life issues?

❧ What progress do you still need to make in the way you are handling your life issues?

Moving Toward Greater Usefulness

It's difficult to stand on the riverbank facing your stream...your challenge...and take a step forward when everything in your human nature wants to retreat to safety, comfort, and the familiar. But God asks you to move forward, to walk with Him *through* your trials.

What Number One problem did you list on page 57?

As you move through this exercise, see how each stepping-stone will help you move ahead!

Stepping-stone #1—How does this step help you in your current trial?

Stepping-stone #2—How does this step help you grow in maturity?

Stepping-stone #3—How can you "let" God do His work in your trial? Also note the three benefits you enjoy when you faithfully take this step.

According to James 5:7-11, what are some ways to let endurance or patience have its perfect work in you?

According to Psalms 37:7 and 40:1, what are some ways to let endurance or patience have its perfect work in you?

According to Matthew 10:22 and Galatians 6:9, what are some ways to let endurance or patience have its perfect work in you?

Seven Ways to Fail God's Tests

Reflect on your obedience to God's plan for you to face your trials and mature spiritually. As you work through the ways people fail God's tests, pay attention to any failures in your past and present. Make "How I can improve" notes as you go.

1. *Resist.* In what way or ways can you identify with Jonah's resistance?

How I can improve:

2. *Retreat.* In what way or ways have you, like Elijah, retreated from a test, a trial, or a challenge that came your way?

How I can improve:

–Taking a Step Forward–

Read this section in your book again. Write out the step or steps you were asked to take to reach greater maturity…to become a mature woman. Feel free to add any additional steps or ideas you think of.

As you consider the contents of this chapter and the maturity you gain as a result of your trials, place a check mark by the step or steps you will take today. What difference do you think taking this step(s) will make in your growth?

Keep on keeping on!

10

Making Decisions that Develop Greatness

❧

*Let endurance have its perfect result,
so that you may be perfect and complete,
lacking in nothing.*
JAMES 1:4 NASB

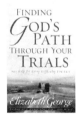

Read chapter 10, "Making Decisions that Develop Greatness," in *Finding God's Path Through Your Trials.* Note any new truths or challenges that stand out to you.

God has wisdom and practical help for you as you face your everyday difficulties, whether they're surprises or ongoing challenges. What is the Number One problem you face today? Write it down and add what instructions God has for you.

Before you continue with the seven ways to fail God's tests, read James 1:4 again. For review, write out the first two ways to fail God's tests we discussed in the last chapter.

#1 _____

#2 _____

3. *Resent.* In what way or ways have you, like Sarah, resented a person, a test, a trial, or a challenge that came your way?

How I can improve:

4. *Denial.* In what way or ways have you, like Peter, denied a weakness while in a test, a trial, or a challenge that came your way?

How I can improve:

5. *Comparison.* In what way or ways have you, like Peter, compared yourself with others while facing a test, a trial, or a challenge that came your way?

How I can improve:

−Taking a Step Forward−

Read this section in your book again. Write out the step or steps you were asked to take to reach greater maturity…to become a mature woman. Feel free to add any additional steps or ideas you think of.

As you consider the contents of this chapter and the maturity you gain as a result of your trials, place a check mark by the step or steps you will take today. What difference do you think taking this step(s) will make in your growth?

Keep on keeping on!

11

Dealing with Roadblocks

*Perseverance must finish its work so that
you may be mature and complete,
not lacking anything.*

JAMES 1:4 NIV

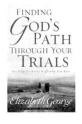

Read chapter 11, "Dealing with Roadblocks," in
Finding God's Path Through Your Trials. Note any
new truths or challenges that stand out to you.

God has wisdom and practical help for you as you face your
everyday difficulties, whether they're surprises or ongoing challenges. What is the Number One problem you face today? Write
it down and add what instructions God has for you.

Before you continue, read James 1:4 again. Now write out the five ways to fail God's tests we've looked at so far.

  #1 _____

  #2 _____

  #3 _____

  #4 _____

  #5 _____

Dealing with Roadblocks to Progress

As you dream of being a mature and useful woman to your family, friends, neighbors, those in your church, and at work, what roadblocks have you identified?

  6. *Pride.* Using a dictionary, write out a definition of pride.

  In what way or ways have you exhibited pride while facing a test, a trial, or a challenge that came your way?

How do the examples from Paul's times of testing instruct you for making it through your testing?

7. *Deception.* Look at these scriptures in your Bible and note what they say about deception. Also write down any solutions given:

Proverbs 14:14-15—

Jeremiah 17:9-10—

1 John 1:8-10—

In what way or ways have you deceived yourself while facing a test, a trial, or a challenge that came your way?

How I can improve:

Letting God Work in You

By now you know you are to let God work in you, to yield to Him and His plans without resistance. Look in your dictionary and write out a definition of the following verbs. Then, once again, note what areas you'd like to improve in.

let—

defer—

yield—

submit—

allow—

How I can improve:

—Taking a Step Forward—

Read this section in your book again. Write out the step or steps you were asked to take to reach greater maturity...to become a mature woman. Feel free to add any additional steps or ideas you think of.

As you consider the contents of this chapter and the maturity you gain as a result of your trials, place a check mark by the step or steps you will take today. What difference do you think taking this step(s) will make in your growth?

Keep on keeping on!

12

Experiencing God's Power and Perfection

❧

*So let [endurance] grow, for when your
endurance is fully developed, you will be strong
in character and ready for anything.*

JAMES 1:4 NLT

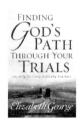

Read chapter 12, "Experiencing God's Power and Perfection," in *Finding God's Path Through Your Trials*. Note any new truths or challenges that stand out to you.

God has wisdom and practical help for you as you face your everyday difficulties, whether they're surprises or ongoing challenges. What is the Number One problem you face today? Write it down and add what instructions God has for you.

Letting God Work in Me

Today is a new day! What are you facing in the Trial Department? List three ways you plan to let God work in you through your challenge.

#1—

#2—

#3—

God's Power Revealed

Review God's process for working in the individuals mentioned in this chapter section and write out how these people inspire you.

In the lions' den—

In the fire—

On the altar—

On the cross—

Which lesson is new for you, or a challenge, or one you need to
pay attention to today? Share your plan for greater growth.

How Long Can You Stay?

As you review the brief summary of God's people who stayed in
their trying situations, note any indicators regarding time. Also jot
down how these people encourage you today.

Noah—

Abraham—

Leah—

Ruth—

Abigail—

Susanna Wesley—

Moving Toward Perfection

Write down how the Bible version you use translates the word or term used for these three end results:

1. *Perfect*—

>Matthew 5:48—As you grow to possess this quality, what person will you resemble?

>Philippians 3:12-14—How can you move toward this quality?

>Colossians 4:12—What should one goal of your Christian life be?

>2 Timothy 3:16-17—Name one purpose of the Word of God.

1 Peter 5:10—What must precede perfection?

How do these truths increase your desire for perfection?

To summarize, what is the key to gaining perfection?

2. *Entire*—This word means complete in every part, entire, or whole.

1 Thessalonians 5:23—What did Paul pray for the Thessalonian believers?

Can you think of an area of your life that needs this quality?

3. *Lacking in nothing—*

Titus 3:13—Write out the instructions Paul gave to Titus.

What would happen if these two men left on their trip without all they needed?

What would happen to you as a believer if you started your day or tried to live the Christian life without all you need?

Describe a situation from your life when a trial came and you were not spiritually prepared for it. How did you handle or mishandle it? What decisions did you make afterward?

Based on these three benefits (perfect, entire, lacking in nothing), what should your attitude be toward the next trial you face?

−Taking a Step Forward−

Read this section in your book again. Write out the step or steps you were asked to take to reach greater maturity…to become a mature woman. Feel free to add any additional steps or ideas you think of.

As you consider the contents of this chapter and the maturity you gain as a result of your trials, place a check mark by the step or steps you will take today. What difference do you think taking this step(s) will make in your growth?

Keep on keeping on!

13

Finding Strength in God's Grace

※

*And [the Lord] said to me, "My grace is sufficient for you,
for My strength is made perfect in weakness."
Therefore most gladly I will rather boast in my infirmities,
that the power of Christ may rest upon me.*

2 Corinthians 12:9

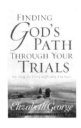

Read chapter 13, "Finding Strength in God's Grace,"
in *Finding God's Path Through Your Trials*. Note any
new truths or challenges that stand out to you.

God has wisdom and practical help for you as you face your
everyday difficulties, whether they're surprises or ongoing challenges. What is the Number One problem you face today? Write
it down and add what instructions God has for you.

HIDING GOD'S WORD IN YOUR HEART

Memorize 2 Corinthians 12:9. Write down how it appears in your favorite Bible version. You may want to look at a few other translations and note any words that differ or help you better understand the meaning of this verse.

REVIEWING YOUR PROGRESS

To view your progress through this book, what three grand qualities can be yours as a result of your tests and trials (see the book's section titles)?

1. A _____ Woman

2. A _____ Woman

3. A _____ Woman

These are outstanding benefits!

Responding to Trials and Tribulations

Take a look at these biblical examples of some wrong ways to respond to your trials:

Escape—Jonah 1:1-3

Explain—Job 38:1-4; 40:1-2

Exit—Genesis 12:10-13

Which has been your favorite? What will you do differently next time?

Describe how each of these better ways to respond to your trials could be used today.

Be joyful—

Believe—

Bend—

Finding Strength in Weakness

Read 2 Corinthians 12:1-10.

Who was interacting with the apostle Paul (verse 8)?

What was the condition of Paul's suffering (verse 7)?

What had brought about this condition (verses 1-4)?

What first right step did Paul take (verse 8)?

What was the answer Paul received (verse 9)?

Staying on God's Path

Look again in your dictionary for definitions of the word "sufficient." Note them here.

Think about your own life and struggles. What are some of the
sufferings you've experienced (from the past or present)?

How does God's clear response to Paul in his suffering
encourage you in yours?

Do you believe God's grace is sufficient for your suffering? Why or why not?

What difference would believing the truth of God's all-sufficient grace extended to you make as you walk through your problems?

Recounting God's Grace

Read this section in your book again. Which situation and person (other than Jesus) can you most identify with and why?

How are you encouraged by God's grace in your circumstances today?

—Taking a Step Forward—

Read this section in your book again. Write out the step or steps you were asked to take to tap into God's might...to become a mighty woman. Feel free to add any additional steps or ideas you think of.

As you consider the contents of this chapter and the mighty power you gain as a result of your trials, place a check mark by the step or steps you will take today. What difference do you think taking this step(s) will make in your growth?

Be strong in His might!

14

Counting on God's Power

∂❦

And [the Lord] has said to me, "My grace is sufficient for you,
for power is perfected in weakness."
Most gladly, therefore, I will rather boast about my weaknesses,
so that the power of Christ may dwell in me.

2 CORINTHIANS 12:9 NASB

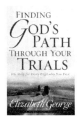

Read chapter 14, "Counting on God's Power," in *Finding God's Path Through Your Trials*. Note any new truths or challenges that stand out to you.

God has wisdom and practical help for you as you face your everyday difficulties, whether they're surprises or ongoing challenges. What is the Number One problem you face today? Write it down and add what instructions God has for you.

Gaining Something Better

Paul prayed three times for God to remove his "thorn in the flesh," yet Paul's pain remained. But he gained something more significant than pain relief. What did he gain (2 Corinthians 12:9)?

How does Paul's model for handling his problem—praying, accepting, and glorying—instruct you?

Putting Weakness to Work

What two conditions are laid side by side in 2 Corinthians 12:9?

God's _____

is _____

in man's/your _____.

How is Isaiah 40:29-31 an example of this truth?

According to Paul's prayer in Ephesians 3:16, how is strength accomplished in weakness?

How did the Old Testament saints find strength according to Hebrews 11:33-34?

Putting God's Strength to Work at Home

Recall a time when you faced a seemingly impossible task or challenge at home that you wanted to give in and give up, yet God's strength came to your rescue. Or maybe you're facing such a time now? Jot down the situation and your thoughts about it.

How did or can God help you, encourage you, strengthen you, and assist you in your daily duties at home?

Or maybe a situation at work or in a relationship is your Number One problem. How can you be strong in the Lord and access the power of His might?

The Scope of Life's Challenges

Share a few of the hardships you've encountered or are encountering right now.

Read the following two scriptures.

> And [God] said to me, "My grace is sufficient for you, for My strength is made perfect in weakness." Therefore most gladly I will rather boast in my infirmities, that the power of Christ may rest upon me (2 Corinthians 12:9).

> But I rejoiced in the Lord greatly that now at last your care for me has flourished again; though you surely did care, but you lacked opportunity (Philippians 4:10).

In light of these verses, how can the fact of God's strength in your weakness and Paul's example of rejoicing in God's provision encourage you and enable you in your current struggle?

—Taking a Step Forward—

Read this section in your book again. Write out the step or steps you were asked to take to tap into God's might...to become a mighty woman. Feel free to add any additional steps or ideas you think of.

As you consider the contents of this chapter and the mighty power you gain as a result of your trials, place a check mark by the step or steps you will take today. What difference do you think taking this step(s) will make in your growth?

Be strong in His might!

15

Drawing on God's Might

֍

But [God] said to me, "My grace is sufficient for you,
for my power is made perfect in weakness."
Therefore I will boast all the more gladly about my
weaknesses, so that Christ's power may rest on me.
That is why, for Christ's sake, I delight in weeknesses, in
insults, in hardships, in persecutions, in difficulties.
For when I am weak, then I am strong.
2 CORINTHIANS 12:9-10 NIV

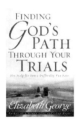 Read chapter 15, "Drawing on God's Might," in *Finding God's Path Through Your Trials*. Note any new truths or challenges that stand out to you.

God has wisdom and practical help for you as you face your everyday difficulties, whether they're surprises or ongoing challenges. What is the Number One problem you face today? Write it down and add what instructions God has for you.

Acknowledging Your Trials

A sign of Christian maturity is acknowledging your difficulties and finding God's strength in your weaknesses. Read 2 Corinthians 4:8-9 and list the four weaknesses Paul identified...and God's strength provided...in each weakness.

We are...   **but not...**

1.

2.

3.

4.

Read through 2 Corinthians 11:23-27. To which of Paul's sufferings do you relate?

What example of strength and weakness does Paul cite in 2 Corinthians 13:3-4?

How was weakness exhibited?

How was power exhibited?

According to these verses, how are you weak?

And how are you powerful?

Responding to God's Grace

Read the first half of 2 Corinthians 12:9 and note here what is said of...

God's grace—

God's strength—

Next read the second half of this verse.

What was Paul's response to God's grace?

How is the power of Christ described?

In this chapter three responses to God's grace and power were suggested:

❧ *Glory in them!*

How are you finding joy in your frailties and infirmities? And are you "boasting" in them?

❧ *Glory in Christ's covering!*

How are you experiencing God's overshadowing presence and power in your weakness?

❧ *Glory in Christ's strength!*

When you are weak, you are strong! How are you witnessing God's strength in your strengthlessness?

Witnessing God's Strength in Others

Scan the life stories of these men who experienced great weakness. Note the specific failing of each man and how God provided His strength.

❧ *Samson* (Judges 16:28-30)—

❧ *Elisha* (1 Kings 19:19-21; 2 Kings 2:9)—

❧ *Stephen* (Acts 6:1-8; 7:59-60)—

Can you think of any women in the Bible who experienced great weakness and also God's provision of great strength?

Compile a list of several steps these men and women took to gain God's strength in their weaknesses.

–Taking a Step Forward–

Read this section in your book again. Write out the step or steps you were asked to take to tap into God's might...to become a mighty woman. Feel free to add any additional steps or ideas you think of.

As you consider the contents of this chapter and the mighty power you gain as a result of your trials, place a check mark by the step or steps you will take today. What difference do you think taking this step(s) will make in your growth?

Be strong in His might!

16

Becoming a Work of Art

❦

Since I know it is all for Christ's good,
I am quite content with my weaknesses and with
insults, hardships, persecutions, and calamities.
For when I am weak, then I am strong.

2 Corinthians 12:10 nlt

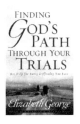

Read chapter 16, "Becoming a Work of Art," in *Finding God's Path Through Your Trials.* Note any new truths or challenges that stand out to you.

God has wisdom and practical help for you as you face your everyday difficulties, whether they're surprises or ongoing challenges. What is the Number One problem you face today? Write it down and add what instructions God has for you.

HIDING GOD'S WORD IN YOUR HEART

Memorize 2 Corinthians 12:10. Write down how it appears in your favorite Bible version. You may want to look at a few other translations and note any words that differ or help you better understand the meaning of this verse.

Understanding God's Process

As you look at 2 Corinthians 12:10, what heart attitude does Paul exhibit regarding his difficulties and suffering?

What made him able to have this response?

Like needlework, painting, or sculpting, there is a process involved in creating a work of art. What is God's process for transforming His people—including you—into masterpieces?

How are you responding to the fact that God is at work in *you,* producing a work of art in *you* by means of your Number One problem—and any and all your other problems?

What difference should this make in how you view your trials and tribulations?

Now look at the five kinds of suffering mentioned by Paul in 2 Corinthians 12:10. Consider how they are perfecting you.

Perfecting Involves Infirmities

Write down the words other Bible versions use for "infirmities."

Jot down a definition for "infirmity" from a dictionary.

What further insights do these scriptures give regarding infirmities?

Luke 5:15—

Luke 7:21—

Luke 8:2—

Share one of your experiences with infirmity.

Perfecting Involves Reproaches
Write down what words other Bible versions use instead of "reproaches."

Jot down a definition for "reproach" from a dictionary.

What further insights do these scriptures give regarding reproaches?
Hebrews 10:32-33—

Share your experience with a reproach.

Perfecting Involves Needs

Write down the words other Bible versions use for "needs."

Jot down a definition for "need" from a dictionary.

What further insights do these scriptures give regarding needs?

Acts 20:34—

2 Corinthians 6:4—

Share your experience with a need.

Perfecting Involves Persecutions

Write down the words other Bible versions use for "persecutions."

Jot down a definition for "persecution" from a dictionary.

What further insights do these scriptures give regarding persecutions?

2 Thessalonians 1:4—

2 Timothy 3:10-11—

Share your experience with a persecution.

Perfecting Involves Distresses

Write down the words other Bible versions use for "distresses."

Jot down a definition for "distress" from a dictionary.

What further insights do you find in 2 Corinthians 6:4-5 regarding distresses?

Share your experience with a distress.

Putting Everything Together

How does 2 Corinthians 12:9 and 10...

...encourage you?

...strengthen you?

...challenge you?

...instruct you?

...change you?

Read the words to the hymn *He Giveth More Grace* by Annie Flint again. Reflect on the truths that God gives you grace for your burdens, strength for your work, mercy for your afflictions, peace in your trials, *and* His limitless love. How do your resources in God further your desire and resolve to stay on His path through your trials?

—Taking a Step Forward—

Read this section in your book again. Write out the
step or steps you were asked to take to tap into God's
might...to become a mighty woman. Feel free to add
any additional steps or ideas you think of.

As you consider the contents of this chapter and the
mighty power you gain as a result of your trials, place
a check mark by the step or steps you will take today.
What difference do you think taking this step(s) will
make in your growth?

Be strong in His might!

17

Enduring Difficult Times

*No temptation has overtaken you except such as is common to man;
but God is faithful, who will not allow you to be tempted
beyond what you are able, but with the temptation
will also make the way of escape, that you may be able to bear it.*

1 CORINTHIANS 10:13

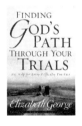

Read chapter 17, "Enduring Difficult Times," in *Finding God's Path Through Your Trials*. Note any new truths or challenges that stand out to you.

God has wisdom and practical help for you as you face your everyday difficulties, whether they're surprises or ongoing challenges. What is the Number One problem you face today? Write it down and add what instructions God has for you.

Hiding God's Word in Your Heart

Memorize 1 Corinthians 10:13. Write down how it appears in your favorite Bible version. You may want to look at a few other translations and note any words that differ or help you better understand the meaning of this verse.

Examining Trials and Temptations

Scan 1 Corinthians 10:1-12 and note some of the many ways God's people were blessed.

How did they fall short when tempted by everyday life situations and trials?

Do you see yourself in any of their failures? Make notes for change!

What lessons can you learn from the Israelites about…

…how easy it is to forget to remember God's goodness?

...how trials can tempt you to sin against God?

What lesson—or warning—does verse 12 have for you?

Accepting Temptation

Spend a few minutes in review.

James 1:2—What does James tell us about the reality of trials?

1 Peter 4:12—What does Peter tell us about the reality of trials?

1 Corinthians 10:13—What does Paul tell us about the reality of trials or temptations?

❧ How does this knowledge about the reality of trials change your response to the trials, tests, and temptations that come your way daily?

Responding to Temptation

Think about the variety of ways we can deal with temptation. Give a brief description of each response below and note the level of maturity or immaturity each represents.

a crybaby—

a brat—

a teen—

an adult—

Which best describes your usual response and why? Again, make notes for change.

❧ What did the Israelites do, according to 1 Corinthians 10:1-12, when tested? How would you describe their level of spiritual maturity, their trust in God?

Preparing for Temptation

Temptation in itself is not sin. It is yielding to temptation that becomes sin. God gives you means for preparing for and withstanding temptation. What do these scriptures tell you about standing strong and resisting temptation?

❧ Proverbs 4:14-15—

❧ Matthew 26:41—

❧ 2 Corinthians 12:9—

❧ Ephesians 6:10-13—

❧ Hebrews 12:1—

❧ James 1:12—

❧ 1 John 4:4—

Planning for Temptation

First Corinthians 10:13 guarantees there will always be a way out of temptation, always a way *not* to give in to sin. Consider these ways of resisting temptation. God will help you...

❧ recognize people and situations that give you trouble;

❧ run from anything you know is wrong;

❧ choose to do only what is right;

❧ pray for His help; and

❧ seek friends who love God and can support you when you are tempted.*

Once again make notes of what you can do to resist temptation in your situation.

Staying Positive

How do these promises from God give you a more positive outlook on your tests and temptations?

1 Corinthians 10:13—

---

* Grant Osborne, gen. ed., *Life Application Bible Commentary—1 & 2 Corinthians* (Wheaton IL: Tyndale House Publishers, Inc., 1999), p. 143.

James 1:3—

James 1:4—

Look at these words from Jesus to His disciples and us. What did He promise?

John 16:33—

John 17:13-15—

How do the promises of God help you...

—follow His instructions?

—stay positive while you do?

–Taking a Step Forward–

Read this section in your book again. Write out the step or steps you were asked to take to endure (be patient) in your trials...and to be a woman at peace. Feel free to add any additional steps or ideas you think of.

As you consider the contents of this chapter and the endurance and peace God gives you for making it through your trials, place a check mark by the step or steps you will take today. What difference do you think taking this step(s) will make in your growth?

Be watching and praying!

18

There Is Nothing New Under the Sun

*No temptation has overtaken you but such as is common to man;
and God is faithful, who will not allow you to be tempted
beyond what you are able,
but with the temptation will provide the way of escape also,
so that you will be able to bear it.*

1 Corinthians 10:13 NASB

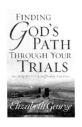

Read chapter 18, "There Is Nothing New Under the Sun," in *Finding God's Path Through Your Trials*. Note any new truths or challenges that stand out to you.

God has wisdom and practical help for you as you face your everyday difficulties, whether they're surprises or ongoing challenges. What is the Number One problem you face today? Write it down and add what instructions God has for you.

What's a Woman to Do?

Make your own list of issues to face and needs (yours and others') to meet in the upcoming week. That's right, look at the next seven days of your life and anticipate what is in store for you (as far as you know anyway).

❧ Before you get too overwhelmed, read 1 Corinthians 10:13 again. Write out the two "answers" to the question asked in this section of your book:

—We understand and accept…

—We realize…

What assurances—and hope!—do these answers give you for your coming week?

Nothing Is Unique

As stated in the book, 1 Corinthians 10:13 tells us in no uncertain terms that no believer is exempt from trials and no trial is unique. In fact, for thousands of years millions of people have faced the same trials you face.

What is the absolute worst problem you are facing other than having too much to do, and how does the truth that nothing is unique put it into perspective...into God's perspective?

❧ To begin dealing with your problem, how do these scriptures help?

Matthew 6:34—

John 16:33—

Philippians 4:6-7—

Philippians 4:13—

Hebrews 2:18—

Hebrews 4:15-16—

2 Peter 1:3—

Now, for today, choose your favorite verse for approaching
and managing the major test or temptation that is right in front
of you.

Hearing God's Good News

Do you agree or disagree that knowing your trials or temptations
are common is good news? And why?

Do you agree or disagree that God can help you endure through
any temptation you ever face? And why?

Do you agree or disagree that because your trials are common,
it stands to reason there are solutions and advice to be gained
from others? And why?

Handling Problems God's Way

Enjoy these many options God has given you for handling your problems and temptations in the right way—His way!

❧ Proverbs 3:6—

❧ Proverbs 24:6—

❧ Proverbs 28:26—

❧ Ephesians 6:12-13—

❧ James 1:5—

-Taking a Step Forward-

Read this section in your book again. Write out the step or steps you were asked to take to endure (be patient) in your trials...and to be a woman at peace. Feel free to add any additional steps or ideas you think of.

As you consider the contents of this chapter and the endurance and peace God gives you for making it through your trials, place a check mark by the step or steps you will take today. What difference do you think taking this step(s) will make in your growth?

Be watching and praying!

Becoming an Enduring Woman

19

Trusting in God's Faithfulness

No temptation has seized you except what is common to man.
And God is faithful; he will not let you be tempted
beyond what you can bear.
But when you are tempted, he will also provide a way out
so that you can stand up under it.

1 CORINTHIANS 10:13 NIV

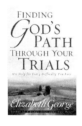

Read chapter 19, "Trusting in God's Faithfulness," in
Finding God's Path Through Your Trials. Note any
new truths or challenges that stand out to you.

God has wisdom and practical help for you as you face your
everyday difficulties, whether they're surprises or ongoing challenges. What is the Number One problem you face today? Write
it down and add what instructions God has for you.

Focusing on God's Faithfulness

How has God demonstrated His faithfulness as seen in these scriptures?

1 Corinthians 1:9 —

1 Corinthians 10:13 —

1 Thessalonians 5:24 —

2 Thessalonians 3:3 —

Hebrews 10:23 —

1 Peter 4:19 —

Counting on God's Faithful Keeping

Look at these facts about God in your Bible and jot down the blessings He extends to you in His faithfulness.

Psalm 91:11 —

Isaiah 26:3-4 —

1 Corinthians 10:13 —

2 Timothy 1:12 —

Jude 24 —

Counting on God's Perfect Timing

Review Romans 5:6, Psalm 31:15, and Ecclesiastes 3:1-8. Write out what impresses you most about God's perfect timing. Also include an instance when you witnessed His perfect timing in your life.

Counting on God's Provision

Enjoy scanning Exodus 14. Write out what impresses you most about God's provision for His people when they are up against a trial. Include a time when you witnessed His perfect provision in giving you a way to escape.

Counting on God's Perfect Knowledge

Scan Daniel 3. Write out what impresses you most about God's perfect knowledge. Add an instance when you witnessed His perfect knowledge of your limits when you were tempted.

Counting on God's Perfect Compassion

Recall Jeremiah's obedience to deliver God's message to His people—people who never paid attention to Jeremiah's preaching and sought to destroy him. What tribute did Jeremiah pay to God and His compassion in Lamentations 3:22-24?

Write out what impresses you most about God's mercy. Share an instance when you witnessed His perfect compassion during a time you were tempted to feel sorry for yourself or give up.

Counting on God's Faithfulness

You have already looked at numerous scriptures concerning God's faithfulness. How has this mini-study of this attribute of your heavenly Father bolstered your courage to trust in Him when you are tried, tested, or tempted?

—Taking a Step Forward—

Read this section in your book again. Write out the step or steps you were asked to take to endure (be patient) in your trials...and to be a woman at peace. Feel free to add any additional steps or ideas you think of.

As you consider the contents of this chapter and the endurance and peace God gives you for making it through your trials, place a check mark by the step or steps you will take today. What difference do you think taking this step(s) will make in your growth?

Be watching and praying!

20

Triumphing over Temptation

*The temptations that come into your life are no different from
what others experience. And God is faithful.
He will keep the temptation from becoming so strong
that you can't stand up against it.
When you are tempted, he will show you a way out
so that you will not give in to it.*

1 Corinthians 10:13 nlt

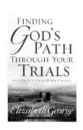

Read chapter 20, "Triumphing over Temptation," in
Finding God's Path Through Your Trials. Note any
new truths or challenges that stand out to you.

God has wisdom and practical help for you as you face your
everyday difficulties, whether they're surprises or ongoing challenges. What is the Number One problem you face today? Write
it down and add what instructions God has for you.

Factoring in God's Faithfulness

Take one more look at 1 Corinthians 10:13 in your favorite version
of the Bible. List what you now know:

❧ Trials are _____.

❧ God is _____.

Promise #1—State this promise in your own words.

How did these people endure their trials and temptations? Note
what the temptation was and how God enabled and encouraged each of them.

Shadrach, Meshach, and Abed-nego (Daniel 3)—

Jesus (Matthew 4)—

Jesus (Luke 22)—

Stephen (Acts 7)—

Promise #2—State this promise in your own words, and then fill in the blanks below.

My role is to _____ in my trials.

God's role is to _____.

What does 2 Peter 2:9 tell you about God and your temptations?

How does this encourage you as you face your trials and temptations?

Two Women in Trials

Briefly describe each of these two women's situations and how they dealt with their temptations.

Sarah—

Elizabeth—

What lessons do these two women teach you about handling
your present problems...and your future ones?

Letting God Work

In chapter 18 in this Growth and Study Guide, under the heading
"What's a Woman to Do," you were asked to make a list of issues
you were facing and the needs of you and others that had to
be met in your upcoming week. Share how your impossible-to-
imagine-and-cope-with-week turned out.

In what ways were you faithful to stay with your commitments?

In what ways did you witness God's faithfulness to:

❧ enable you in your situations and commitments?

❧ make a way of escape...just at the right moment?

How did you:

❧ grow to trust God even more?

❧ grow in your staying power and endurance?

❧ grow in your understanding of God's enablement and intervention when you are tempted?

—Taking a Step Forward—

Read this section in your book again. Write out the step or steps you were asked to take to endure (be patient) in your trials...and to be a woman at peace. Feel free to add any additional steps or ideas you think of.

As you consider the contents of this chapter and the endurance and peace God gives you for making it through your trials, place a check mark by the step or steps you will take today. What difference do you think taking this step(s) will make in your growth?

Be watching and praying!

21

Gaining Something Grand

> *Be anxious for nothing, but in everything*
> *by prayer and supplication, with thanksgiving,*
> *let your requests be made known to God.*
> PHILIPPIANS 4:6

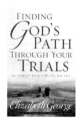

Read chapter 21, "Gaining Something Grand," in *Finding God's Path Through Your Trials*. Note any new truths or challenges that stand out to you.

God has wisdom and practical help for you as you face your everyday difficulties, whether they're surprises or ongoing challenges. What is the Number One problem you face today? Write it down and add what instructions God has for you.

HIDING GOD'S WORD IN YOUR HEART

Memorize Philippians 4:6. Write down how it appears in your favorite Bible version. You may want to look at a few other translations and note any words that differ or help you better understand the meaning of this verse.

Recapping Our Journey

To recap, write out the five section titles of the types of women highlighted in this book. Then in ten words or less, create your own definition or description for each type of woman.

1.

2.

3.

4.

5.

Now recap your growth in each area. For instance, how have you seen yourself change? How has your spiritual growth advanced? How do you currently see yourself handling your trials, tests, and temptations? Take some time to notice your progress and give thanks to God.

Handling All Your Trials

At the beginning of this chapter I quoted some "worry" statistics. When it comes to worrying about life, about trials, about finances, about your days, about your loved ones, which percentage group did you envision yourself qualifying for?

Look now at Philippians 4:6.

❧ First, the negative...

What did the apostle Paul say you are *not* to do about your problems and difficulties?

Read Matthew 6:25-34 and list the concerns in life that can produce worry. List the reasons Jesus gives about why worrying is wrong.

Concern   **Why you are not to worry**

❧ How do you recognize worry and anxiety in yourself in the following giveaway behaviors? Be specific in each area.

We question—

We are obsessed—

We are consumed—

We are distracted—

✤ Next, the positive...

Instead of worrying, what does Paul advise in Philippians 4:6?

What does he say the result will be (verse 7)?

What does Peter advise (1 Peter 5:7)?

Comprehending the Breadth of Prayer

Prayer contains the following elements. Look up the scriptures to gain better insights into the depth and breadth of prayer.

✤ *Prayer*—Quickly note the specifics about prayer found in these scriptures.

Matthew 21:22—

Luke 1:13—

Luke 6:12—

Luke 22:44—

Acts 6:4—

Acts 12:5—

Romans 12:12—

1 Corinthians 7:5—

Ephesians 6:18—

1 Peter 4:7—

❧ *Supplication*—Look up the word "supplication" in a dictionary and jot down a short definition.

Note any specifics about "supplication" from these verses:

Acts 1:14—

Ephesians 6:18 (used two times)—

❧ *Thanksgiving*—Note any specifics about "thanksgiving" from these verses:

2 Corinthians 4:15—

2 Corinthians 9:11—

Colossians 2:7—

Colossians 4:2—

1 Timothy 4:3-4—

Revelation 7:12—

❧ *Requests*—Pick the meaning for "requests" you like best as it relates to your prayer life:

___ to ask   ___ to crave

___ to beg   ___ to desire

___ to call for   ___ to request

Consider again your worries and worrying habits. In a world filled with stress and tension, challenge and difficulty, how can your life be marked with God's peace according to Philippians 4:6 and 7?

What decisions do you need to make about your prayer life to gain something grand—to gain God's peace?

—Taking a Step Forward—

Read this section in your book again. Write out the step or steps you were asked to take to enjoy God's perfect peace...to become a peaceful woman. Feel free to add any additional steps or ideas you think of.

As you consider the contents of this chapter and the peace you gain as a result of praying in and during your trials, place a check mark by the step or steps you will take today. What difference do you think taking this step(s) will make in your growth?

Pray without ceasing!

Leading a Bible Study Discussion Group

※

What a privilege it is to lead a Bible study! And what joy and excitement await you as you delve into the Word of God and help others to discover its life-changing truths. If God has called you to lead a Bible study group, I know you'll be spending much time in prayer and planning and giving much thought to being an effective leader. I also know that taking the time to read through the following tips will help you navigate the challenges of leading a Bible study discussion group and enjoy the effort and opportunity.

The Leader's Roles

As a Bible study group leader, you'll find your role changing back and forth from *leader* to *cheerleader* to *lover* to *referee* during the course of a session.

Since you're the leader, group members will look to you to be the *leader* guiding them through the material. So be well prepared. In fact, be over-prepared so that you know the material better than any group member does. Start your study early in the week and let its message simmer all week long. (You might even work several lessons ahead so that you have in mind the big picture and the overall direction of the study.) Be ready to share some additional gems that your group members wouldn't have discovered on their own. That extra insight from your study time — or that comment from a wise Bible teacher or scholar, that clever saying, that keen observation from another believer, and even an appropriate joke — adds an element of fun and keeps Bible study from becoming routine, monotonous, and dry.

Next, be ready to be the group's *cheerleader.* Your energy and enthusiasm for the task at hand can be contagious. It can also stimulate people to get more involved in their personal study as well as in the group discussion.

Third, be the *lover,* the one who shows a genuine concern for the members of the group. You're the one who will establish the atmosphere of the group. If you laugh and have fun, the group members will laugh and have fun. If you hug, they will hug. If you care, they will care. If you share, they will share. If you love, they will love. So pray every day to love the women God has placed in your group. Ask Him to show you how to love them with His love.

Finally, as the leader, you'll need to be the *referee* on occasion. That means making sure everyone has an equal opportunity to speak. That's easier to do when you operate under the assumption that every member of the group has something worthwhile to contribute. So, trusting that the Lord has taught each person during the week, act on that assumption.

Leader, cheerleader, lover, and referee — these four roles of the leader may make the task seem overwhelming. But that's not bad if it keeps you on your knees praying for your group.

A Good Start

Beginning on time, greeting people warmly, and opening in prayer gets the study off to a good start. Know what you want to have happen during your time together and make sure those things get done. That kind of order means comfort for those involved.

Establish a format and let the group members know what that format is. People appreciate being in a Bible study that focuses on the Bible. So keep the discussion on the topic and move the group through the questions. Tangents are often hard to avoid — and even harder to rein in. So be sure to focus on the answers to questions about the specific passage at hand. After all, the purpose of the group is Bible study!

Finally, as someone has accurately observed, "Personal growth is one of the by-products of any effective small group. This growth is achieved when people are recognized and accepted by others. The more friendliness, mutual trust, respect, and warmth exhibited, the more likely that the member will find pleasure in the group, and, too, the more likely she will work hard toward the accomplishment of the group's goals. The effective leader will strive to reinforce desirable traits" (source unknown).

A Dozen Helpful Tips

Here is a list of helpful suggestions for leading a Bible study discussion group:

1. Arrive early, ready to focus fully on others and give of yourself. If you have to do any last-minute preparation, review, re-grouping, or praying, do it in the car. Don't dash in, breathless, harried, late, still tweaking your plans.

2. Check out your meeting place in advance. Do you have everything you need — tables, enough chairs, a blackboard, hymnals if you plan to sing, coffee, etc.?

3. Greet each person warmly by name as she arrives. After all, you've been praying for these women all week long, so let each VIP know that you're glad she's arrived.

4. Use name tags for at least the first two or three weeks.

5. Start on time no matter what — even if only one person is there!

6. Develop a pleasant but firm opening statement. You might say, "This lesson was great! Let's get started so we can enjoy all of it!" or "Let's pray before we begin our lesson."

7. Read the questions, but don't hesitate to reword them on occasion. Rather than reading an entire paragraph of instructions, for instance, you might say, "Question 1 asks us to list some ways that Christ displayed humility. Lisa, please share one way Christ displayed humility."

8. Summarize or paraphrase the answers given. Doing so will keep the discussion focused on the topic, eliminate digressions, help avoid or clear up any misunderstandings of the text, and keep each group member aware of what the others are saying.

9. Keep moving and don't add any of your own questions to the discussion time. It's important to get through the study guide questions. So if a cut-and-dried answer is called for, you don't need to comment with anything other than a "thank you." But when the question asks for an opinion or an application (for instance, "How

can this truth help us in our marriages?" or "How do *you* find time for your quiet time?"), let all who want to contribute do so.

10. Affirm each person who contributes, especially if the contribution was very personal, painful to share, or a quiet person's rare statement. Acknowledge everyone who shares a hero by saying something like "Thank you for sharing that insight from your own life" or "We certainly appreciate what God has taught you. Thank you for letting us in on it."

11. Watch your watch, put a clock right in front of you, or consider using a timer. Pace the discussion so that you meet your cut-off time, especially if you want time to pray. Stop at the designated time even if you haven't finished the lesson. Remember that everyone has worked through the study once; you are simply going over it again.

12. End on time. You can only make friends with your group members by ending on time or even a little early! Besides, members of your group have the next item on their agenda to attend to — picking up children from the nursery, babysitter, or school; heading home to tend to matters there; running errands; getting to bed; or spending some time with their husbands. So let them out *on time!*

Five Common Problems

In any group, you can anticipate certain problems. Here are some common ones that can arise, along with helpful solutions:

1. *The incomplete lesson* — Right from the start, establish the policy that if someone has not done the lesson, it is best for her not to answer the questions. But do try to include her responses to questions that ask for opinions or experiences. Everyone can share some thoughts in reply to a question like "Reflect on what you know about both athletic and spiritual training, and then share what you consider to be the essential elements of training oneself in godliness."

2. *The gossip* — The Bible clearly states that gossiping is wrong, so you don't want to allow it in your group. Set a high and strict standard by saying, "I am not comfortable with this conversation," or "We [not *you*] are gossiping, ladies. Let's move on."

3. *The talkative member* — Here are three scenarios and some possible solutions for each.

   a. The problem talker may be talking because she has done her homework and is excited about something she has to share. She may also know more about the subject than the others and, if you cut her off, the rest of the group may suffer.

   SOLUTION: Respond with a comment like: "Sarah, you are making very valuable contributions. Let's see if we can get some reactions from the others," or "I know Sarah can answer this. She's really done her homework. How about some of the rest of you?"

   b. The talkative member may be talking because she has *not* done her homework and wants to contribute, but she has no boundaries.

SOLUTION: Establish at the first meeting that those who have not done the lesson do not contribute except on opinion or application questions. You may need to repeat this guideline at the beginning of each session.

c. The talkative member may want to be heard whether or not she has anything worthwhile to contribute.

SOLUTION: After subtle reminders, be more direct, saying, "Betty, I know you would like to share your ideas, but let's give others a chance. I'll call on you later."

4. *The quiet member* — Here are two scenarios and possible solutions.

a. The quiet member wants the floor but somehow can't get the chance to share.

SOLUTION: Clear the path for the quiet member by first watching for clues that she wants to speak (moving to the edge of her seat, looking as if she wants to speak, perhaps even starting to say something) and then saying, "Just a second. I think Chris wants to say something." Then, of course, make her a hero!

b. The quiet member simply doesn't want the floor.

SOLUTION: "Chris, what answer do you have on question 2?" or "Chris, what do you think about…?" Usually after a shy person has contributed a few times, she will become more confident and more ready to share. Your role is to provide an opportunity where there is *no* risk of a wrong answer. But occasionally a group member will tell you that she would rather not be called on.

Honor her request, but from time to time ask her privately if she feels ready to contribute to the group discussions.

In fact, give all your group members the right to pass. During your first meeting, explain that any time a group member does not care to share an answer, she may simply say, "I pass." You'll want to repeat this policy at the beginning of every group session.

5. *The wrong answer* — Never tell a group member that she has given a wrong answer, but at the same time never let a wrong answer go by.

SOLUTION: Either ask if someone else has a different answer or ask additional questions that will cause the right answer to emerge. As the women get closer to the right answer, say, "We're getting warmer! Keep thinking! We're almost there!"

Learning from Experience

Immediately after each Bible study session, evaluate the group discussion time using this checklist. You may also want a member of your group (or an assistant or trainee or outside observer) to evaluate you periodically.

May God strengthen — and encourage! — you as you assist others in the discovery of His many wonderful truths.

Personal Notes

Personal Notes

Personal Notes

Personal Notes

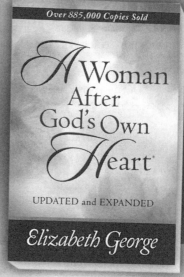

A Woman After God's Own Heart® Study Series

Bible Studies for Busy Women

God wrote the Bible to change hearts and lives. Every study in this series is written with that in mind—and is especially focused on helping Christian women know how God desires for them to live.

—Elizabeth George

Sharing wisdom gleaned from more than 20 years as a women's Bible study teacher, Elizabeth has prepared insightful lessons that can be completed in 15 to 20 minutes per day. Each lesson includes thought-provoking questions, insights, Bible-study tips, instructions for leading a discussion group, and a "heart response" section to make the Bible passage more personal.

A Woman After God's Own Heart

Living with Passion and Purpose

LUKE

Elizabeth George

978-0-7369-0816-0

Becoming a Woman of Beauty & Strength

ESTHER

Elizabeth George

978-0-7369-0489-6

Putting On a Gentle & Quiet Spirit

1 PETER

Elizabeth George

978-0-7369-0290-8

Discovering the Treasures of a Godly Woman

PROVERBS 31

Elizabeth George

978-0-7369-0818-4

Nurturing a Heart of Humility

CHARACTER STUDIES MARY

Elizabeth George

978-0-7369-0300-4

Walking in God's Promises

CHARACTER STUDIES SARAH

Elizabeth George

978-0-7369-0301-1

Experiencing God's Peace

PHILIPPIANS

Elizabeth George

978-0-7369-0289-2

Pursuing Godliness

1 TIMOTHY

Elizabeth George

978-0-7369-0665-4

Cultivating a Life of Character

JUDGES/RUTH

Elizabeth George

978-0-7369-0498-8

Growing in Wisdom & Faith

JAMES

Elizabeth George

978-0-7369-0490-2

HARVEST HOUSE PUBLISHERS
EUGENE, OREGON 97402
www.harvesthousepublishers.com

A Mom After God's Own Heart

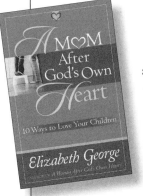

Catch God's Heart for your children

You want to raise children who are happy and successful, and who follow after God. But how do you do that in this day of hectic schedules packed with friends, schoolwork, sports, video games, cell phones, and the internet? The first thing is to begin right now. Today. Share your love, your faith, and your values with your children.

With biblical wisdom and plenty of encouragement, Elizabeth George offers time-proven ideas and valuable suggestions to help you nurture children of all ages in the Lord. You'll discover...

- ❧ Easy-to-implement principles that make parenting enjoyable and effective
- ❧ Specific ways you can teach your children that God loves and cares for them
- ❧ "Heart Response" sections that help you apply the principles to your life
- ❧ "Little Choices" you can put into practice immediately to make a big impact
- ❧ Special parenting insights and strategies from a Christian dad

God has put you in a unique situation where you have tremendous influence in the lives of others. Be a mom after God's own heart! Help your children—no matter what their ages—experience God's love, God's blessings, and God's provisions.

For more in-depth and personal or group study
A Mom After God's Own Heart Growth and Study Guide

The Remarkable Women of the Bible

Experience God's life-changing power as the women of the Bible experienced it.

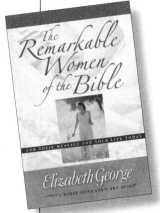

Come and see how God enabled ordinary women to live extraordinary lives! How did He do it? By turning their weaknesses into strengths, their sorrows into joys, and their despair into hope.

This book explores the fascinating lives of these women. Along the way you'll also learn great truths about God...

- From Eve you'll see God is faithful even when you fail

- From Sarah you'll find God always keeps His promises

- From Rebekah you'll discover God has a plan for your life

- From Mary you'll learn God will always care for you.

What made these women—and many others—so remarkable? They loved God passionately, looked to Him in life's daily challenges, and yielded to His transforming grace. And you can enjoy God's miraculous work in your life today...by following in their footsteps!

Books by Elizabeth George

- Beautiful in God's Eyes
- Finding God's Path Through Your Trials
- Life Management for Busy Women
- Loving God with All Your Mind
- A Mom After God's Own Heart
- Powerful Promises for Every Woman
- The Remarkable Women of the Bible
- Small Changes for a Better Life
- A Wife After God's Own Heart
- A Woman After God's Own Heart®
- A Woman After God's Own Heart® Deluxe Edition
- A Woman After God's Own Heart®—A Daily Devotional
- A Woman After God's Own Heart® Collection
- A Woman's Call to Prayer
- A Woman's High Calling
- A Woman's Walk with God
- A Young Woman After God's Own Heart
- A Young Woman's Call to Prayer
- A Young Woman's Walk with God

Children's Books

- God's Wisdom for Little Girls
- A Little Girl After God's Own Heart

Study Guides

- Beautiful in God's Eyes Growth & Study Guide
- Finding God's Path Through Your Trials Growth & Study Guide
- Life Management for Busy Women Growth & Study Guide
- Loving God with All Your Mind Growth & Study Guide
- A Mom After God's Own Heart Growth & Study Guide
- The Remarkable Women of the Bible Growth & Study Guide
- Small Changes for a Better Life Growth & Study Guide
- A Wife After God's Own Heart Growth & Study Guide
- A Woman After God's Own Heart® Growth & Study Guide
- A Woman's Call to Prayer Growth & Study Guide
- A Woman's High Calling Growth & Study Guide
- A Woman's Walk with God Growth & Study Guide

Books by Jim & Elizabeth George

- God Loves His Precious Children
- God's Wisdom for Little Boys
- A Little Boy After God's Own Heart

Books by Jim George

- The Bare Bones Bible™ Handbook
- God's Man of Influence
- A Husband After God's Own Heart
- A Man After God's Own Heart
- The Remarkable Prayers of the Bible
- The Remarkable Prayers of the Bible Growth & Study Guide
- What God Wants to Do for You
- A Young Man After God's Own Heart

About the Author

Elizabeth George is a bestselling author who has more than four million books in print. She is a popular speaker at Christian women's events. Her passion is to teach the Bible in a way that changes women's lives. For information about Elizabeth's speaking ministry, to sign up for her mailings, or to purchase her books visit her website:

www.ElizabethGeorge.com

Toll-free: 1-800-542-4611

Elizabeth George
PO Box 2879
Belfair, WA 98528